CHILDREN'S ENCYCLOPEDIA
THE WORLD OF KNOWLEDGE
CHEMISTRY

Manasvi Vohra

Published by:

F-2/16, Ansari road, Daryaganj, New Delhi-110002
☎ 23240026, 23240027 • *Fax:* 011-23240028
Email: info@vspublishers.com • *Website:* www.vspublishers.com

Regional Office : Hyderabad
5-1-707/1, Brij Bhawan (Beside Central Bank of India Lane)
Bank Street, Koti, Hyderabad - 500 095
☎ 040-24737290
E-mail: vspublishershyd@gmail.com

Branch Office : Mumbai
Jaywant Industrial Estate, 2nd Floor-222, Tardeo Road
Opposite Sobo Central, Mumbai - 400 034
☎ 022-23510736
E-mail: vspublishersmum@gmail.com

Follow us on:

All books available at **www.vspublishers.com**

© Copyright: V&S PUBLISHERS
Edition 2017

The Copyright of this book, as well as all matter contained herein (including illustrations) rests with the Publishers. No person shall copy the name of the book, its title design, matter and illustrations in any form and in any language, totally or partially or in any distorted form. Anybody doing so shall face legal action and will be responsible for damages.

Printed at: Repro Knowledgecast Ltd., Thane.

PUBLISHER'S NOTE

V&S Publishers is glad to announce the launch of a unique, set of 12 books under the head, *Children's Encyclopedia – The World of Knowledge.* The set of 12 books namely – *Physices, Chemistry, Space Science, General Sceince, Life Science, Human Body, Electronics & Communications, Scientists, Inventions & Discoveries, Transportation, The Earth, and GK (General Knowledge)* has been especially developed keeping in mind the students and children of all age groups, particularly from 6 to 14 years of age. Our main aim is to arouse the interest and solve the queries of the school children regarding the various and diverse topics of Science and help them master the subject thoroughly.

In the book, *Chemistry*, the author has broadly dealt with some interesting and fascinating Scientific facts which focusses mainly on *Matter, Properties of Matter, Changing States of Matter, Mass, Volume and Density, Atoms, Molecules, Elements, Properties of Elements, Chemical Reactions and Changes, Acids and Bases and so on .....*

Each chapter is followed by a section called **Quick Facts** that contains a set of interesting and fascinating facts about the topics already discussed in the chapter. There are also **Exercises** compiled at the end of the book followed by a **Glossary** of difficult words and scientific terms to make the book complete and comprehensive.

Quick Facts

- The coldest temperature possible is absolute zero, or – 273°C, when molecules stop moving.

Though our aim is to be flawless, but errors might have crept in inadvertently. So we request our esteemed readers to read the book thoroughly and offer valuable suggestions wherever necessary to improve and enhance the quality of the book. Hope it interests you all and serves its purpose well.

CONTENTS

CHEMISTRY

Chapter 1 : Matter   9
Chapter 2 : Properties of Matter   13
Chapter 3 : Changing States   17
Chapter 4 : Mass, Volume and Density 21

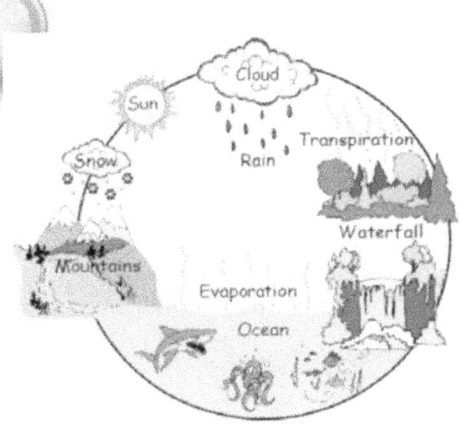

Chapter 5 : Atoms   25
Chapter 6 : Molecules   29
Chapter 7 : Elements   33
Chapter 8 : Properties of Elements   38

Chapter 9 : Compounds and Mixtures   44
Chapter 10 : Reactions and Changes   48
Chapter 11 : Irreversible and Reversible Changes 52
Chapter 12 : Acids and Bases   56

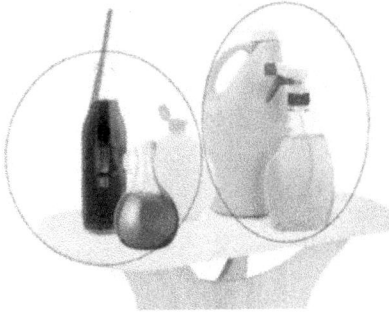

Chapter 13 : Solids   60
Chapter 14 : Liquids   65
Chapter 15 : Gases   69
Exercises   73
Glossary   77

CHEMISTRY

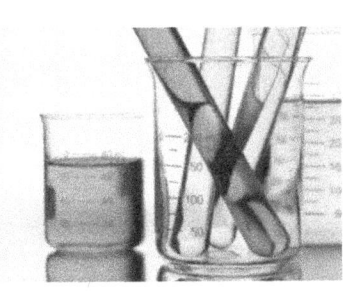

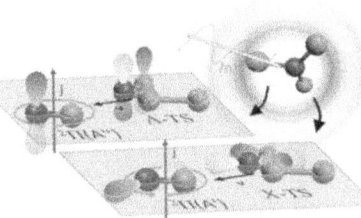

Chapter - 1

MATTER

Everything around us is made up of matter. A 'matter' is any type of material and anything that has mass, and takes up space. Matter is also related to light and *electromagnetic radiation*. It includes things we can see as well as we cannot see, such as tables, chairs, boxes, men, women, plants, animals, etc., are matter or objects that we can see, but gases like Hydrogen (H_2), Oxygen (O_2), Nitrogen(N_2), etc., are matter that we cannot see, yet they occupy space and volume. Hence, Matter is anything made up of atoms and molecules that has mass or weight and occupies space or volume.

An Astronaut in Space

A Table and Chairs

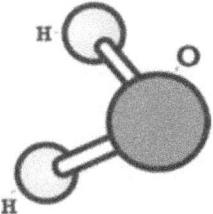
Two Hydrogen Atoms and A Molecule of Oxygen combine to form H_2O or Water Molecule

Two Atoms of Hydrogen and one atom of Oxygen combine to form a molecule of Water or H_2O.

Types of Matter

There are **four** main types of matter. All of these behave differently because the particles in their make up move in different ways.

1. Solid

A solid has a definite shape and volume. A solid object is rigid. The atoms and molecules in a solid are tightly packed together and are not compressible.

Atoms/Molecules in a Solid

Examples of solids are: All things that are hard to touch and cannot be compressed like rock, wood, television, computer, etc.

Stone (A Solid)

2. Liquid

A liquid does not have a definite shape, but they do have a definite volume. A liquid takes the shape of its container. Its molecules are further apart than solids. They change their shape by flowing. Since the atoms and molecules touch each other, the density of a liquid is close to that of a solid.

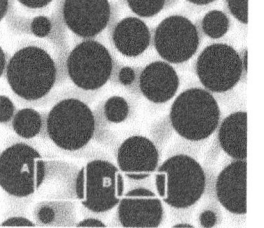 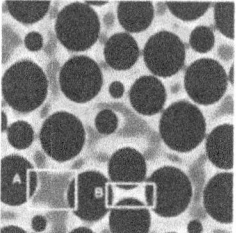

Atoms/Molecules in a Liquid

Water (A Liquid)

Examples of liquids are: All things that take the shape of their container like water, oil, honey, etc.

3. Gases

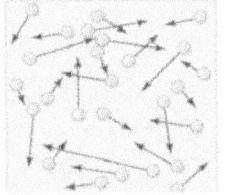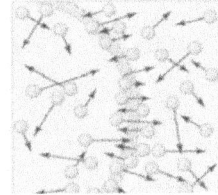

Gases have neither a definite shape nor a definite volume. If confined, gases take the shape of their container

Atoms/Molecules in a Gas

and if left out, then they spread out in the atmosphere. The atoms and molecules of gases are spread out resulting in a very low density and have enough energy to overcome attractive forces.

Examples of gases are: Oxygen, Hydrogen, Helium, Nitrogen, Air, etc. We cannot see gases until we see their container or they have a particular colour. A way to see a gas is by blowing up a balloon. The air we blow into it take the shape of the balloon and it blows up.

A Balloon filled with Air

4. Plasma

Plasma has neither a definite shape nor a definite volume. Plasma can be achieved by heating and ionizing a gas. Free electrical charges make plasma electrically conductive. Plasma has some properties of liquids and some of gases. It is the most common state of matter in our universe and most of it is not visible.

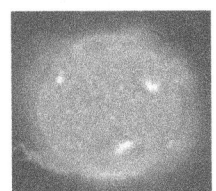

Plasma

Examples of plasma are: It exists inside the sun, stars are made up of plasma, lightning is also a type of plasma. You can also find plasma inside *fluorescent lights*, *lightning* and *neon signs*.

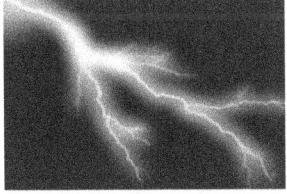

Lightning

Bose-Einstein Condensate

Two scientists, Satyendra Bose and Albert Einstein had predicted this fifth state of matter in 1920. At that time, they did not have the equipment and facilities to create it. In 1995, two scientists, Cornell and Weiman finally created this new state of matter.

Bose-Einstein condensate can be said to be the opposite of plasma. Plasma have super hot and super excited atoms, while the atoms of Bose-Einstein condensate are totally opposites, they are super-unexcited and super-cold atoms. At a certain temperature, near zero atoms clump together and they no longer remain many atoms, but take on the same qualities and become one *blob*. Cornell and Weiman did this with an element called *Rubidium*.

Quick Facts

- A place where there is no matter at all is called a vacuum. The best example of a vacuum is the space between stars.

- Particles in a gas vibrate and move freely at high speeds. Particles in a liquid vibrate, move about, and slide past each other, and particles in a solid vibrate (jiggle) but generally do not move from place to place.

- Changes, such as pressure and temperature, can alter the states of Matter, whether Solids, Liquids or Gases.

- Most everyday matter, occurs as mixtures which are combinations of two or more substances. For example: In water, two atoms of Hydrogen combine with one atom of Oxygen to form the Chemical Formula: H_2O.

- When solid matter changes to a liquid, it is called melting and when liquid changes to a gas, it is called sublimation.

- When liquids change to a gas, it is also called vaporization and when liquids change to solids, it is called freezing. When a gas changes to plasma, it is called ionization.

Chapter - 2

PROPERTIES OF MATTER

There are so many types of materials around us, all have different properties. By properties, we mean some materials are *colourful*, some are *brittle*, some are *very hard* and some may be *transparent*. All these different features are called *properties*.

There are many different properties on which materials can be classified:

1. Boiling Point

Boiling point is the hottest a liquid can get before it changes into a gas. When a liquid is heated, it reaches a temperature, where vapour from inside the liquid rises. Once the liquid starts to boil, the temperature remains constant until all of the liquid has been converted into gas.

Water Boiling in a Pan

2. Freezing Point

The freezing point is the temperature at which a liquid becomes a solid. When a liquid is cooled, it reaches a temperature, where its atoms and molecules become tightly packed like that of a solid.

Although liquids can be frozen beyond their freezing points, and then they are called *supercooled*.

Ice Cubes in an Ice Tray

3. Melting Point

The melting point is the temperature at which a solid turns into a liquid. When a solid is heated, it reaches a temperature, where its atoms and molecules start to move around and it turns into a liquid.

Lighted Candles with Wax Melting

4. Conductivity

Conductivity is how well can a material let electricity or heat travel through it.

Heat is transferred from a hot body to a cold one and electricity is transferred by a charged body to a neutral one.

A Utensil on a Gas

Materials that are good at conduction are called **conductors**. Materials that do not conduct heat or electricity are called **insulators**. Aluminium or steel are good conductors of heat and are therefore used in cooking utensils. Copper or aluminium are good conductors of electricity and therefore are used to make electrical wires.

Copper Wire (Conductor)

5. Flammability

Flammability is how easily or quickly a material catches fire. We use materials as per their flammability. For cooking, we always use materials that are not flammable like aluminium which is a

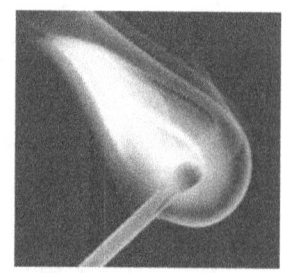
A Matchstick Burning

good conductor of heat but does not burn. If we use a cloth to cook food, then it will catch fire. In the opposite case, if we want to light a fire, we will use a material that burns like wood.

6. Flexibility

A Rubber Band

An Eraser

Flexibility is how easily a material can be bent. It is the rigidity of an object, the point till which it resists bending. Rubber, elastic, etc can be easily bent while wood or iron cannot be bent.

7. Compressibility

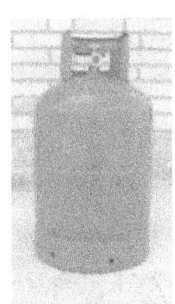

A LPG Cylinder

Compressibility means how much can the volume of a material be changed when pressure is applied on it. Since solids and liquids have a definite volume, therefore it is very difficult to compress them. However, gases can be easily compressed and are used in compressed forms in our houses as *LPG or cooking gas.*

8. Transparency

Glass Window (Transparency)

It is the property that determines how well a material lets light pass through it. Glass, water and air let light pass through them very easily.

Solids like wood, iron and steel do not let light pass through them. Materials that let light pass through them appear transparent, i.e., they appear to be colourless.

9. Viscosity

A River Flowing Smoothly

Viscosity or stickiness is the property which makes a liquid flow smoothly or slowly. If the viscosity is less, the liquid will flow freely and smoothly and if the viscosity is high, the liquid will flow slowly. Water has a low viscosity and flows smoothly while the lava from a volcano has a high viscosity.

Volcano has High Viscosity

10. Malleability

Malleability is the property of a solid. It determines how easily can the solid be shaped without breaking. The most common solid known for its malleability is gold. Different shapes, designs and patterns are made with gold and used as jewellery. This can happen only because gold is very malleable.

Gold is Malleable

Quick Facts

- Substances, which break easily, are called brittle substances and substances, which can be beaten into sheets, are called malleable substances.
- Substances, which can be drawn into wires, are ductile substances.
- Substances that change their shape and size when an external force is applied and which regain their original form when the force is removed, are elastic substances.
- Substances, which absorb moisture from the air, are deliquescent. Substances that lose moisture are efflorescent.
- The process of intermixing of molecules is called diffusion.
- Opaque substances do not allow light to pass through. Transparent substances allow light to pass through. Translucent substances allow some light to pass through.

Chapter - 3

CHANGING STATES OF MATTER

When solids get hot enough, *they melt and turn into liquids*. When liquids get cold enough, *they freeze and turn into solids*. When liquids become hot enough, they turn into steam or gas. At certain temperatures, all substances change their states. *Gases* can be turned into *plasma* with the help of very cold temperatures.

Matter changes its state through *melting, freezing, evaporation* and *condensation*. Heat is the most common way that changes the state of matter. Heat when applied to a solid changes it to a liquid. Heat changes a liquid to a gas. Heat is also involved in evaporating water from clothes that are hung out to dry. Condensation results in gases changing or converting into liquids.

Freezing

When liquids are put into cold temperatures, their atoms become tightly packed together and they turn into solids. Water turns into ice when we keep it in the freezer. All liquids have different freezing points. It we keep both water and honey into the freezer, they will freeze at different temperatures.

Ice Cubes

Melting

When solids are heated, after a certain temperature, their atoms become loosely packed and they turn into liquids. Most solids have high melting points, therefore a large amount of heat is needed to melt them. In factories, iron is heated and melted to make different instruments with it.

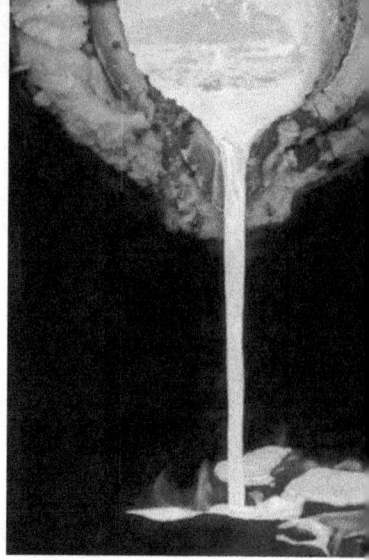
Motten Iron

Evaporation

When *we heat a liquid, it begins to evaporate.* Water evaporates in the form of steam. We can see this steam when we boil water in a pan in our houses. Another common example of evaporation is when we hang our clothes out in the sun to dry. The heat from the sun slowly evaporates all the water still present in our clothes and our clothes become dry.

Water Evaporating from Wet Clothes

Condensation

Condensation occurs when a gas comes in contact with a cool surface. The lower temperature changes the form of a gas into liquid. In summers, when we leave out a bottle of cold water, we can see water droplets being formed on its outside. This is the air around that is changing in liquid form because of the cold bottle surface.

Water exists in all three states on our planet. It is also one of the reasons that life exists on earth. In liquid state, we use it as water for drinking,

Plastic Bottles with Water Droplets on the Outside

washing and various other purposes. In solid state, we use water as ice and in gaseous state, we use it as steam.

A Digital Thermometer

Do it Yourself

Take a few ice cubes from the freezer and put them in a pan on the stove. As it gets heated, the ice will change into liquid water. If you keep applying the heat, the water will begin to boil. As the water begins to boil, you will be able to see water vapours rising from the pan.

Ice Cubes

Now cover the pan with a plate. After some time, when you remove the plate, you will see water droplets on it which were formed because steam changed into water on touching the cooler plate. This water in liquid form can again be frozen by putting it in the freezer.

Boiling Water

Changing States of Water in Nature

It is fun and interesting to see the changing states of water because we can try it at home. But water also changes its state on a very large scale on the earth. Glaciers that melt in summers bring water to the rivers. The heat from the sun evaporates water from the rivers and the oceans into the

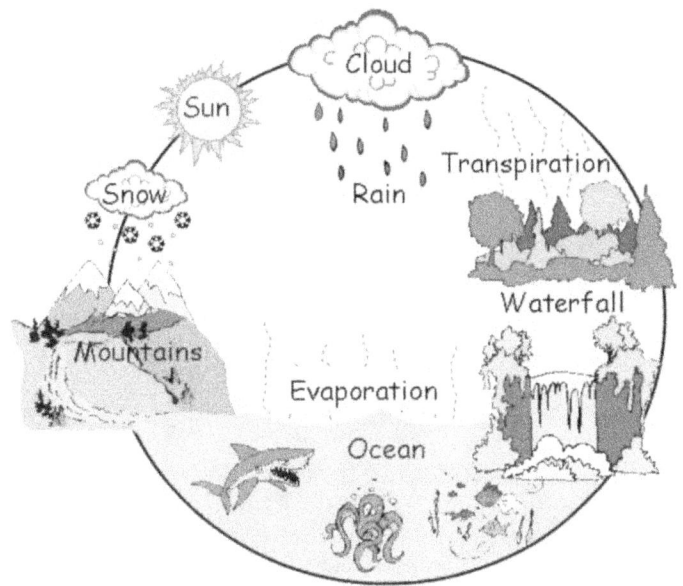

Water Cycle in Nature

atmosphere. Then when it rains, the water returns back to the earth and in winters, the water present on the mountains freezes back to a solid forming ice or snow.

Quick Facts

- Mercury is the only metal that exists in liquid form in room temperature. This is because its melting point is low. Mercury is most often used in thermometers to measure the body temperature.
- Stars, including the sun, are made of matter in the plasma state. In fact, most of the matter in the Universe, particularly in the Galaxy exists in the plasma state! The states of matter can also be called the phases of matter.
- The state of matter of a substance depends on how fast its particles move and how strong the attraction is between its atoms and molecules.
- Solids maintain their shapes and volume. The particles of the substance vibrate in place. The vibration isn't strong enough to overcome the attraction of the particles and cause them to separate. As a result, the forces between the particles cause them to lock together.

Chapter - 4

MASS, VOLUME AND DENSITY

Mass

Mass is the amount of matter an object has. It is measured in grams. *Mass is different from weight.* Mass measures the matter in an object, whereas weight is the measurement of the pull of gravity of an object. Mass is measured using a balance comparing the known amount of matter to the unknown amount of matter, whereas, weight is measured by a scale. The mass of an object does not change when the location of an object changes, but the weight of an object changes according to its location.

Volume

Volume is the amount of space an object occupies. The space can be occupied by any substance like solid, liquid or gas. The volume of an object is calculated by the amount of liquid displacement. *Volume is expressed in cubic centimetres.*

Density

The density of a material helps to distinguish it from other materials. Density is calculated by the formula: Density = Mass/Volume. Density is measured in mass per unit volume. Therefore, $D = \dfrac{M}{V}$

Every substance has a different density. Density is defined as the relative heaviness of an object with a constant volume. It also refers to how closely or tightly are the atoms of a substance packed. For example, Styrofoam and Stone both are solids, but they do not have the same density.

A Piece of Styrofoam

A Piece of Rock

Measuring Mass, Volume and Density

Mass

Mass is measured using a triple balance beam. It is called so because it has three beams that allow you to move known masses along the beam. It is unaffected by gravity and gives a true measure of the mass of an object.

A Triple Balance Beam

Weighing a Dice

There are many other types of balances. Scientists often use different types of balances to calculate a very small amount of mass.

Volume

There are two types of objects, *regular* and *irregular*. Regular objects have systematical dimensions, whereas, irregular objects have irregular dimensions. If you want to measure the volume of a regular object, it is simply length times height times weight. The formula is Volume = Length × Height × Weight (V = L×W×H) and is expressed in cubic centimetres.

The volume of irregular objects is measured by the displacement of a liquid. This is done in laboratories using a graduated cylinder.

Do it Yourself

Take a glass bowl and fill it half way. Mark the level of the water. Now take a small stone and put it inside the water. You will notice a rise in the water level. Mark the new level. The difference between both the levels is the volume of the stone.

A graduated cylinder measures the volume of an irregular object in the same way. It has proper markings on its sides so that the measurement is accurate.

Glass Bowl with Stones in It

Density

As we read earlier, the formula for measuring density is Density = Mass/Volume. So for measuring the density of any object, you should first measure their mass and volume. Once you have both the quantities, you can find out the density using the above formula.

Quick Facts

- Weightlessness can be felt when a person falls freely and suddenly. For example: The weight of an object comes from the fact that a person is supported by the floor or the chair, etc. If this support is removed, then the person falls freely and he feels weightlessness. Therefore, weightlessness refers to a state of being in a free fall in which there is no support.

- While on a rollercoaster, if there is a sudden fall at high speed, then you can feel this weightlessness. This happens because suddenly all support is taken away and the person is almost falling freely.

- Objects with mass are attracted to each other, and towards the Earth's surface. This is known as gravity.
- Density measurements are used when weight and weight distribution are important. This may include the construction of ships, buildings, airplanes and other modes of transportation. Density measurements are also useful when determining how much force is required to move a liquid through piping or tubing. Density also comes into play when packaging engineers design squirt bottles for things such as ketchup and mustard.

Chapter - 5

ATOMS

An atom is the smallest particle that makes up any matter. It is the smallest unit of an element that exhibits all the chemical properties of that *element*. It consists of a tiny, dense, central nucleus made up of *protons* and *neutrons* surrounded by *electrons*.

Some matter is made up of only one kind of atom. The properties of an *element* depend upon the kind of atoms that it is made up of. There are about *112 known kinds of atoms* and therefore, there are around *112 known elements*.

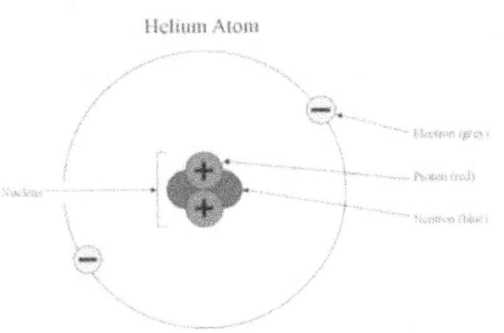

Particles in an Atom

There are three particles present in an atom: **Electrons** which have a **negative charge**, **Protons** which have a **positive charge** and **Neutrons** which have no charge.

Protons and Neutrons are present inside the **nucleus** of an atom. The nucleus is in the centre and contains all the mass of the atom. Electrons are present outside the nucleus. There are equal number of protons and electrons in an atom. Almost all the space inside an atom is empty and the kind of atom is determined by the number of protons in it. This is called the **atomic number**.

Atoms are very small and therefore, cannot be seen through the naked eye. Powerful microscopes are required to know the structure of the atom. Earlier, there were no powerful microscopes, therefore scientists made models of the structure of the atom on paper to study them.

Scientist Observing through a Microscope

Now with the help of new technologies, scientists are finding more about the atom and the models of an atom keep changing. They may keep changing in the future too keeping in mind the advancement in technology.

Chemical Bonding

Most atoms join with other atoms, and this is called chemical bonding. It is a process where atoms and molecules bond together usually to form a new material. The outer electrons' orbit or shell determines which elements or molecules combine and how well they bond together.

Chemical bonding happens through the changes in how electrons are arranged. Some arrangements are stable and some are very unstable. When an atom bonds with another, it usually does so in a way to make the arrangement *stable*.

There are two ways in which chemical bonding happens: either atoms can transfer electrons from one to another or, they can share electrons. An atom can be stable only if there are equal number of protons and electrons in it. The two main types of bonds formed by atoms are:

1. Ionic Bond

An ionic bond is formed when one atom accepts or gives electrons to another atom. Ionic bonds are weaker than covalent bonds. Most of the solid things in the universe, like rocks, use ionic bonds to hold themselves together. *Ionic bonds are formed between metals and non-metals.*

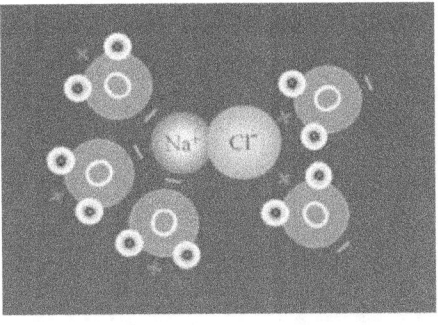

Bonding between $Na^+ + Cl^- = NaCl$ (Common Salt)

During the reaction of sodium and chlorine, sodium loses its one electron to chlorine which results in a positively charged sodium ion and negatively charged chlorine ion.

2. Covalent Bond

In covalent bonding, the atoms are unstable because their outer rings of electrons aren't filled up. When they share electrons with other atoms, these atoms fill up their outer rings and become stable.

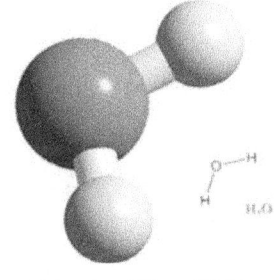

A Molecule of Water (H_2O)

In water, for example, the oxygen atom needs two more electrons to be stable and the hydrogen atoms, each need one. When they form a bond, the oxygen atom shares one electron with each of the hydrogen atoms, and the hydrogen atoms, each share one electron with the oxygen atom.

For every pair of electrons shared, a single covalent bond is formed. Some atoms share multiple pairs of electrons forming multiple covalent bonds.

Quick Facts

- As we all know, an Atom is the smallest particle of an element still having the same chemical properties of the element.

- The first theory of the atom's appearance was made in 1911 by Ernest Rutherford.

- Particles smaller than atoms are called subatomic particles. Electrons, protons and neutrons are the three major subatomic particles. Today scientists understand that protons and neutrons are made of even smaller particles called quarks which are tied together with particles called gluons.

- It is believed that an atom is made of 200 or more than 200 subatomic particles because it is believed that in an atom, there is so much space and electrons take only 1/1000th of the volume. This space may have some more subatomic particles in it.

- An atom can lose electrons, but not protons or neutrons.

- If you split a nuclear atom, it will explode! This fact led to the invention of the Atom Bomb!

Chapter - 6

MOLECULES

A molecule is made up of two or more atoms. *When atoms bond together, they form molecules.* Molecules cannot be seen by the naked eye but they can be seen through an *electron microscope*. Almost everything on earth and other planets is made up of molecules. Also some of the dust in space is made up of molecules.

The shape of the molecules and the way in which they pack together help to explain how different materials behave. The smallest kind of molecule that exists in space is two hydrogen atoms combined together or H_2O. Most of the molecules in space are hydrogen atoms. These combine with other kinds of atoms and form different materials.

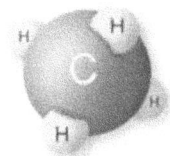
CH_4(Methane)

Two hydrogen atoms combined with one oxygen atom makes water molecule. Hydrogen combined with carbon makes hydrocarbon molecules. Molecules bond with other atoms by ionic and covalent bonding.

Molecules in Different States Melt and Solidify

Molecules are always moving around. When they get heated, they begin to move faster and further. When a solid heats up, its molecules move faster until they break free from each other and move separately. This turns the solid into a liquid.

While, when a liquid cools, its molecules lose energy and become slow. They start sticking to each other, and turn the liquid into a solid.

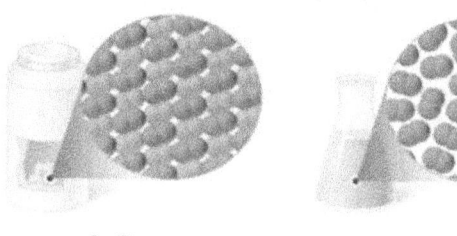

$O_2(S)$ $O_2(L)$

Evaporate and Condense

When a liquid heats up, its molecules start moving faster and further apart until they are moving so fast that they float as gas.

Here O_2 = Oxygen (Element)
S = Solid G = Gas
L = Liquid

 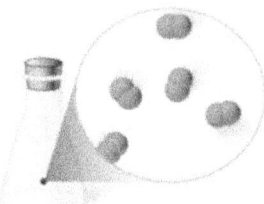

When a gas is cooled, its molecules lose energy and become slow. They then start sticking together and form a liquid.

$O_2(L)$ $O_2(G)$

Diamond and Graphite

Diamond is the hardest natural substance on earth. Each atom in a diamond molecule is joined by strong bonds to four neighbouring atoms and this makes diamond very hard.

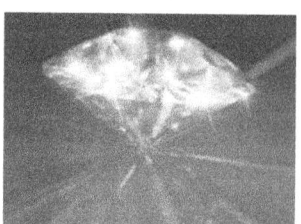

Diamond

Pencils with Graphite

Graphite is also a carbon atom like diamond but it is much softer than diamond. This is because the atoms in graphite are arranged in a different way which makes graphite soft. Each carbon atom in graphite is joined to three neighbouring atoms.

New Materials

Molecules bond with each other in different ways and form new substances. New and different materials are being made by joining two or more molecules. The biggest organic molecule today is the DNA or the Deoxyribonucleic acid. Each molecule of DNA has more than two billion carbon atoms plus other kinds of atoms.

The Planet, Earth

Scientists today make new kinds of molecules in laboratories and factories. Some of the biggest molecules made by man are *plastics*. *Plastics are hydrocarbon molecules*. New molecules are also made in the field of medicine to find cures for diseases.

After the **Big Bang**, when the planets were taking form, most planets were being made of lighter materials. The earth being closer to the sun, was made from heavier molecules like iron. A lot of silicon and other minerals also piled on the earth and made up the rocks of the earth's crust.

Quick Facts

- Molecules are made up of two or more atoms, either of the same element or of two or more different elements, joined by one or more covalent chemical bonds.
- A molecule is two or more atoms bonded together. It is normally the smallest bit of a substance that exists independently.
- According to the kinetic-molecular theory, the molecules of a substance are in constant motion. The state (solid, liquid, or gaseous) in which matter

appears depends on the speed and separation of the molecules in the matter.

- Substances differ according to the structure and composition of their molecules. A molecular compound is represented by its molecular formula; for example, water is represented by the formula, H_2O. A more complex structural formula is sometimes used to show the arrangement of atoms in the molecule.
- The shape of a molecule depends on the arrangement of bonds that hold its atoms together.
- Ammonia or NH_3 molecules are pyramid shaped; some protein molecules are long spirals.
- Compounds only exist as molecules. If the atoms in the molecule of a compound were separated, the compound would cease to exist.
- Diamond is used to cut other hard substances in industries. It is the hardest substance known but it can be destroyed by burning.

Chapter - 7

ELEMENTS

Elements are the building blocks of all matter. When we talk about elements, we are referring to chemical elements. Everything from living things, plants to rocks are made up of elements. So far *117 elements have been discovered*, out of which *94 of them are found naturally*, while the others have been created by scientists in laboratories.

Everything around us is made up of elements in different combinations. The air around us is made up of mostly nitrogen and also elements like oxygen, carbon and a few others. We are made up of mostly *carbon, hydrogen, oxygen and nitrogen.*

Periodic Table

In the periodic table, *elements are arranged by the number of protons in their atoms*. The table looks like a grid and the elements are placed in specific places because of the way they look and act. The rows and columns in the periodic table each mean a different thing.

One row in the periodic table is called a period. The elements in one row have something in common. All the elements in the first row have one *atomic orbital*. In the second row, two atomic orbitals

The Periodic Table

and so on. *The maximum number of atomic orbitals for an element is seven.*

One column of the periodic table is called a group. All the elements in the same group have the same number of electrons in their outer orbital. All elements in the first group have one electron in the outer orbital. Elements in the second group have two electrons in their outer orbital and so on.

The periodic table arranges elements into a pattern so that you can predict their properties based on where they are located in the periodic table.

Metals and Non-Metals

Metals

Most elements are metals. *Metals are separated from non-metals in the periodic table with a zig-zag line.* The properties of metals are: All metals are shiny, and they are good conductors of heat and electricity. They have a high melting point and a high density, and they are malleable and ductile. The are usually solids at room temperature (the exception is mercury). They are opaque and sonorous, i.e., they make a bell like sound when struck.

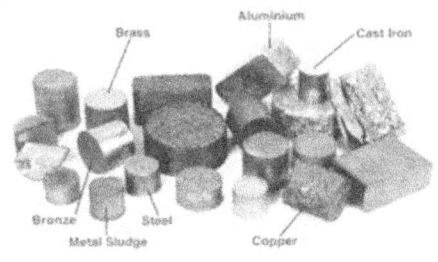
Metals

Non-Metals

Non-metals have the following properties: They do not shine, and they are poor conductors of heat and electricity. They are non-ductile and brittle, may be solid, liquid or gas at room temperature, and they are transparent and are not sonorous.

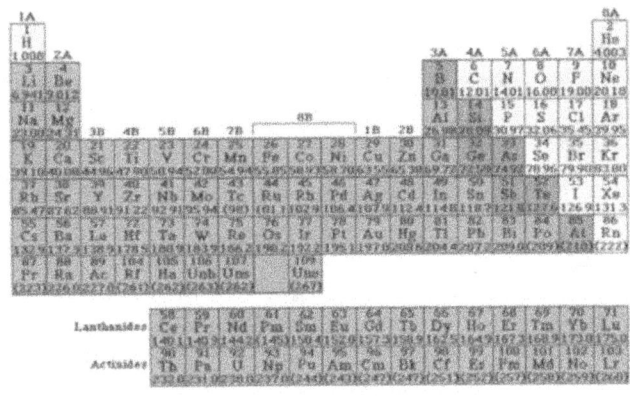
Non-Metals

Uses of Elements

We use a lot of metals in our daily lives. Some metals are also used for specific purposes in laboratories and factories. Elements are used for various useful as well as decorative purposes.

1. Gold

Gold is a precious metal used to make jewellery.

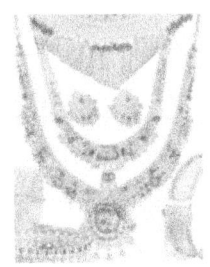
Gold Jewellery

2. Copper

Copper is a good conductor of electricity and is used to make electrical wires.

Electrical Copper Wires

3. Mercury

Mercury is a liquid metal. It is used in dental fillings and in thermometers.

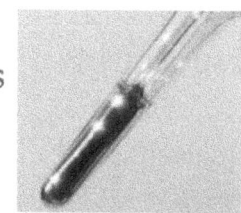
A Mercury Thermometer

4. Iron

Iron is a very strong element. It has many uses. It is also magnetic and is used to make a variety of things from grills, gates to trucks and magnets.

A Grilled Gate

5. Titanium

Titanium is a light-weight metal and it is used in the manufacturing of aeroplanes.

Titanium in Aeroplanes

6. Helium

Helium is a gas used in balloons which makes them float in air because they are lighter than air.

Helium Gas Balloons

7. Chlorine

Chlorine is a *yellow-green gas*. It is used as a *bleach* and also to make *plastics*.

Chlorine Bleach

8. Silicon

Silicon is a non-metal used to make computers and computer chips.

Silicon Computer Chip

9. Sulphur

Sulphur is a *yellow non-metal*. It is used to harden rubber to make tyres.

Sulphur Particles

10. Aluminium

Aluminium is a *soft shiny metal*. It is used to make a number of useful things like aluminium foils, roofs, soft drink cans, aeroplanes, etc.

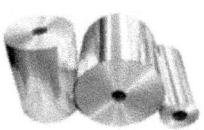
Aluminium Rods

Quick Facts

- Each chemical element on the Periodic Table is arranged according to its atomic number, as based on the periodic law, so that chemical elements with similar properties are in the same column.

- The Periodic Table is simple to use - just look at the symbols for the elements of your choice for additional facts and information, and for an instant comparison of the Atomic Weights, Melting Points, Boiling Points and Mass of a specific element with any other of the elements.

- Nitrogen is the most abundantly found element in the atmosphere. It composes 78 percent of the atmosphere at the ground level, Oxygen comprises about 21 percent and the rest 1 percent consists of all other gases.

Chapter - 8

PROPERTIES OF ELEMENTS

The properties of elements are classified as either **chemical** or **physical**. Chemical properties are observed through a chemical reaction and physical properties are observed by examining a pure sample of the element.

The chemical properties of an element are due to the distribution of electrons that are involved in chemical reactions. A chemical reaction does not affect the atomic nucleus, therefore the atomic number remains the same.

The physical properties of elements can be observed in the collection of atoms and molecules of an element. These include its colour, density, melting point, boiling point, thermal and electrical conductivity, etc.

Elements are grouped in the periodic table according to their properties. The major classification between elements is metals, non-metals and metalloids. Elements that have very similar properties are referred to as **families**. Some families of elements are *halogens*, *inert gases* and *alkali metals*.

Metals, Non-Metals and Metalloids

Metals have properties that you normally associate with a metal in your daily life. Most elements are metals.

Non-metals have properties opposite to those of metals.

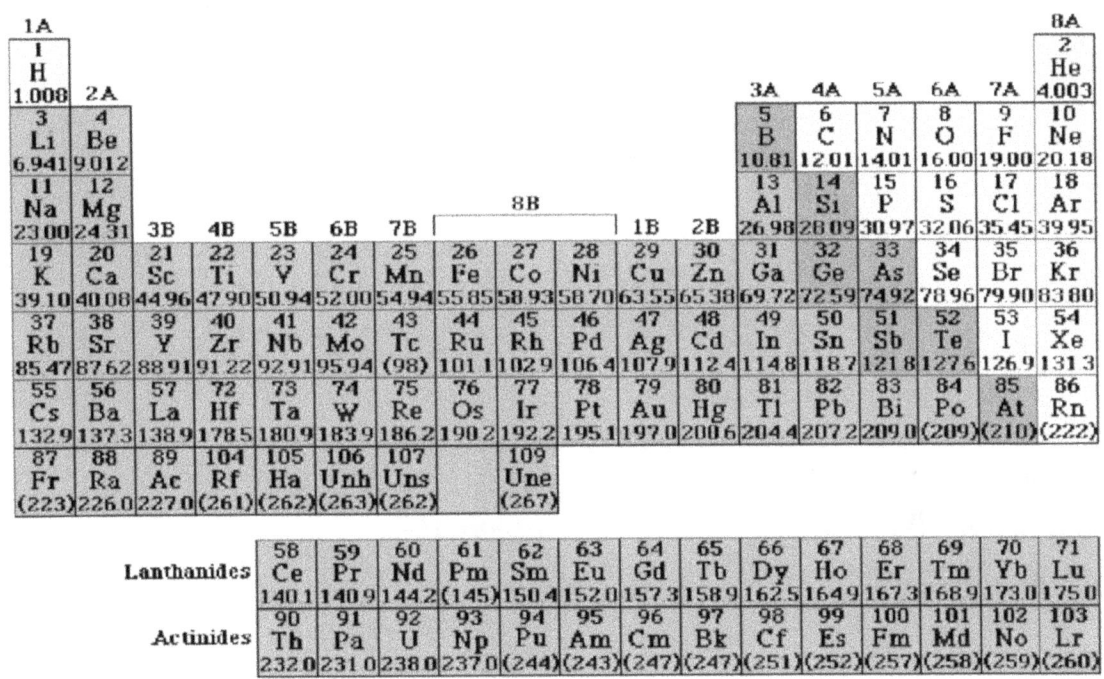

The Periodic Table

Metalloids have properties of both metals and non-metals.

Halogens

Halogens are a particular type of non-metals. There are *five halogen elements:* **Fluorine, Chlorine, Bromine, Iodine** and **Astatine**.

Group	1	2	3	4	5	6	7	8	9	10	11	12	13	14	15	16	17	18
Period 1	1 H																	2 He
2	3 Li	4 Be											5 B	6 C	7 N	8 O	9 F	10 Ne
3	11 Na	12 Mg											13 Al	14 Si	15 P	16 S	17 Cl	18 Ar
4	19 K	20 Ca	21 Sc	22 Ti	23 V	24 Cr	25 Mn	26 Fe	27 Co	28 Ni	29 Cu	30 Zn	31 Ga	32 Ge	33 As	34 Se	35 Br	36 Kr
5	37 Rb	38 Sr	39 Y	40 Zr	41 Nb	42 Mo	43 Tc	44 Ru	45 Rh	46 Pd	47 Ag	48 Cd	49 In	50 Sn	51 Sb	52 Te	53 I	54 Xe
6	55 Cs	56 Ba	57* La	72 Hf	73 Ta	74 W	75 Re	76 Os	77 Ir	78 Pt	79 Au	80 Hg	81 Tl	82 Pb	83 Bi	84 Po	85 At	86 Rn
7	87 Fr	88 Ra	89** Ac	104 Rf	105 Db	106 Sg	107 Bh	108 Hs	109 Mt	110 Ds	111 Rg	112 Cn	113 Uut	114 Uuq	115 Uup	116 Uuh	117 Uus	118 Uuo

Legend:
- Non Metals
- Alkali Metals
- Alkaline Metals
- Transition Metals
- Rare Earth Elements
- Noble Gases
- Metalloids
- Halogens
- Other Metals

*Lanthanides	58 Ce	59 Pr	60 Nd	61 Pm	62 Sm	63 Eu	64 Gd	65 Tb	66 Dy	67 Ho	68 Er	69 Tm	70 Yb	71 Lu
**Actinides	90 Th	91 Pa	92 U	93 Np	94 Pu	95 Am	96 Cm	97 Bk	98 Cf	99 Es	100 Fm	101 Md	102 No	103 Lr

Most halogens are found in small quantities in the earth's crust except for astatine which does not occur naturally.

Halogens are reactive non-metals and have *seven valence electrons or seven electrons in the outermost orbits of their atoms*. All the halogens show variable physical properties. Halogens can be *solid, liquid or gas* at room temperature. Their chemical properties are almost similar. Halogens are very *electronegative,* and *their atoms attract electrons*.

Inert Gases

Inert gases are also called noble gases because they hardly react with other chemicals. The inert gases are *helium, neon, argon, krypton, xenon and radon*.

Inert gases are used by us in many ways. Neon is used in *advertising signs*, and argon is used in *light bulbs*. Helium is used in balloons and to cool things, and xenon is used in *headlights* of new cars. The inert gases are rare in nature, but they are useful too.

Alkali Metals

Metals, such as *lithium, sodium, potassium, rubidium, cesium and francium* are called Alkali Metals. They exhibit some of the properties of metals, but their densities are lower than normal metals. Alkali metals have one electron that is loosely bound. They have low *ionization energy and low electronegativity*. They are highly reactive to other chemicals.

Transition Elements

Transition elements possess most of the properties of normal metals and are therefore, also called *transition metals*. These elements are very hard and have *high melting* and *boiling points*. They are *good conductors of electricity* and are *malleable*. They have *low ionization energies*.

Quick Facts

- Any pure substance or element, under appropriate conditions, can exist in three different states: solids, liquids and gases. States of matter are examples of physical properties of a substance. Other physical properties include appearance (shiny, dull, smooth, rough), odour, electrical conductivity, thermal conductivity, hardness and density, etc.

- Physical changes are changes in outward appearances that do not alter the chemical nature of the substance and produce no new substance. When a chemical change occurs, a new substance is produced. Just like physical properties describe the appearance or intensive properties of a substance, chemical properties describe the set of chemical changes that are possible for that substance or element to form new substances.

- However, the law of mass conservation (conservation of mass) simply states, that there is no detectable change in the total mass of materials when they react chemically (undergo a chemical change) to form new substances.

Chapter - 9

COMPOUNDS AND MIXTURES

When different elements bond together through a chemical reaction, they form **compounds**. Mixtures are formed when elements are mixed together and no bonding takes place.

Compounds

Compounds are chemical unions of separate elements. It is formed when different elements combine together in fixed proportions. The elements do not retain their properties and it is very difficult to separate the elements in a compound.

Water (H_2O) is a Compound

Common Salt (NaCl) is a Compound

Energy is given off or absorbed when a compound is formed and to separate its ingredients also, energy is needed. The creation of a compound depends on a chemical reaction.

Examples of compounds are **pure water (H_2O)**, which is a compound of *oxygen and hydrogen in a fixed proportion*, and **table salt (NaCl)**, which is a compound of sodium and chlorine.

Blast Furnace

Iron oxide (FeO) is a compound of iron and oxygen. To get pure iron, these elements have to be separated and this is done in a blast furnace. Extremely hot air is blasted into the furnace which makes the iron melt. The pure melted iron called the *pig iron* settles at the bottom. Pig iron is transformed into many useful forms of iron.

TYPES OF COMPOUNDS

Ionic Compounds

Ionic compounds are formed when metallic elements from the left side of the periodic table react with the non-metallic elements of the right side of the periodic table. These compounds have high boiling and melting points.

Ionic compounds are generally soluble in water, they are brittle and do not conduct electricity, although in the liquid form, they do conduct electricity.

Molecular Compounds

Molecular compounds are formed when two or more non-metals bond together and form molecules. These generally have low melting and boiling points. Molecular compounds do not conduct electricity in solid or liquid form. Some dissolve in water and some do not.

Mixtures

A mixture is formed when two or more materials join together, where no chemical reaction takes place and no chemical bonding occurs. The components of a mixture retain their original properties and can be separated through physical means.

When a mixture is formed, no energy is either absorbed or given off. Mixtures can be created by mechanical means. Mixtures can be separated through the process of evaporation, filtering or the use of a magnetic force.

Examples of mixtures are air, which is a mixture of many gases, and sea water, which is a mixture of salt and water.

TYPES OF MIXTURES

Solution

Solutions are mixtures that are mixed in even distribution. A simple solution is two substances that are going to be combined. These are called the **solvent** and the **solute**. A solute is the substance to be dissolved and the solvent is the substance that is doing the dissolving. *Example: Sugar and water, here solute is sugar and the solvent is water.*

Suspension

Suspensions are a mixture of two substances, where they do not dissolve completely. The heavier component will settle down if the mixture is left undisturbed or by filtration. The components can be evenly distributed by shaking the mixture, but the solid will ultimately settle down. *Examples of suspensions are sand and water or oil and water.*

Quick Facts

- The composition of a mixture is variable. Each of its components retains its characteristic properties. Its components are easily separated. The relative proportions of the elements in a compound are fixed.

- However, the components of a compound do not retain their individual properties. For example, in table salt or common salt, both sodium and chlorine are poisonous; but their compound, table salt (NaCl) is absolutely essential to life and adds taste to our food. It takes large inputs of energy to separate the components of a compound.

Chapter - 10

REACTIONS AND CHANGES

When in a molecule, the atoms rearrange to form new kinds of molecules, change takes place. There are two types of changes that can happen: *Physical change and Chemical change.*

Chemical Change

Rusting of Iron

A chemical change happens due to a chemical reaction, when chemicals combine in different ways to make new chemicals. Chemical changes take place at the molecular level and produce a new substance. The new substance is different from the original substances that were involved in the change.

Chemical changes can result in molecules combining with each other to form larger molecules or molecules breaking apart to form smaller molecules. The basic structures of the molecules change.

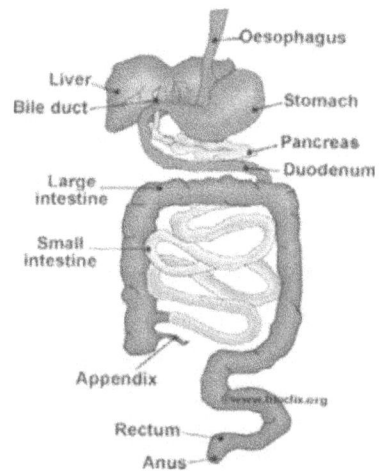

Digestive System in Human Beings

Chemical changes can take a long time to happen or may happen in a few minutes. Rusting of iron takes a long time, while cooking creates chemical reactions in minutes.

Examples of chemical change are burning, cooking, rusting, etc.

Do it Yourself

You can do a chemical reaction by yourself at home. Put some vinegar in a bowl and add baking soda into it. This creates bubbles and fizz. You can make your own volcano by using these ingredients.

Vinegar and Baking Soda

Physical Change

A physical change does not create a new substance. It may change the size, shape or colour of a substance, but does not change its composition.

A Crushed Can

Melting, freezing, condensation, vaporization, etc. are all physical changes that result in the change of the state of the substance.

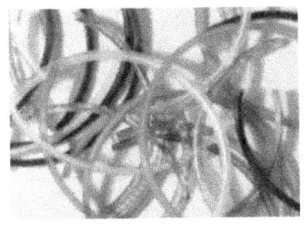
Broken Bangles

The materials involved in a physical change remain the same, even though they make look different after the change takes place. Physical changes do not affect the atomic and molecular structure of a substance. The core properties of substances do not change because physical changes do not affect them.

Examples of physical change are crushing of a tin can, melting of ice, stretching rubber band and breaking of glass.

Snow Melting to form River

Do it Yourself

We do a lot of physical changes everyday. When we cut a piece of paper, it is a physical change because the shape of the paper changes. When we boil water, it is a physical change as the state of water changes. When we add turmeric into water, the colour of water changes. Therefore, this also is a physical change.

Boiling of Water

Physical Change in Humans

Humans also go through a lot of physical changes during the course of life. We grow in height, lose our teeth, cut our hair and nails, colour our hair, etc --all these are physical changes that happen in us.

Growth in Humans

Quick Facts

- The earth also goes through physical changes. The mountains and glaciers move that changes their shapes or formations. The river water and oceans rising are also instances of physical change. Hence, Drought and Floods both are effects of Physical Change.

- Chemical changes take place on the molecular level. A chemical change produces a new substance. Examples of chemical changes include combustion (burning), cooking an egg, rusting of an iron pan, and mixing hydrochloric acid and sodium hydroxide to make salt and water.

- Physical changes are concerned with energy and states of matter. A physical change does not produce a new substance. Changes in state or phase (melting, freezing, vaporization, condensation, sublimation) are physical changes. Examples of physical changes include crushing a can, melting an ice cube, and breaking a bottle.

- A chemical change makes a substance that wasn't there before. There may be clues that a chemical reaction took place, such as light, heat, colour change, gas production, odour, or sound. The starting and ending materials of a physical change are the same, even though they may look different.

Chapter - 11

IRREVERSIBLE AND REVERSIBLE CHANGES

When two substances react and change and cannot be changed back to their original components that is called an *irreversible change*. When two substances can be brought back to their original components after a change, it is called a *reversible change*.

Certain physical changes are reversible, but not all. While most chemical changes are irreversible because they produce a new substance and you cannot get back the original components after the change has occurred.

Irreversible Physical Changes

Do it Yourself

Take a bowl and mix flour and water in it. When we knead dough, it is a physical change because the basic components of both the ingredients, water and flour, remain the same. There is no chemical reaction and thus, no new component is formed.

A Bowl with Kneaded Dough

But you cannot reverse the change and get back flour and water as two separate ingredients. That is why this is an irreversible change.

Some physical changes cannot be reversed. Examples of physical changes that are irreversible are growing up, cooking, burning, rotting of food, etc.

Reversible Physical Change

Some physical changes are reversible. Though you need a method to get back the original ingredients, but it can be done.

Do it Yourself

Take a glass of water and mix some sand in it. The water will turn brownish and a physical change takes place. But if you let the solution stable and untouched for some time, you will notice the sand settling down. Left for a long time, you will notice that a large amount of sand has settled down and the water looks relatively cleaner.

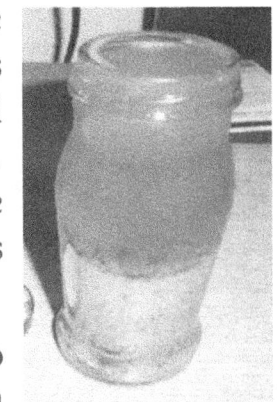

Sand and Water

Now pick the glass slowly and pour the water into another glass leaving the sand behind. This way you have reversed a physical change. You have both the ingredients, water and sand, back and the change has been reversed.

Examples of reversible physical changes are separating salt from water through evaporation, bending a plastic and then straightening it, folding a piece of paper and then unfolding it, etc.

Irreversible Chemical Changes

Chemical changes cannot be reversed. As chemical changes occur at the molecular level, it is almost impossible to reverse them. A new substance in formed through a chemical change and the original components lose their properties.

Many new substances are produced in factories and laboratories using different elements. Substances, such as nylon, polymer, plastic, tin, steel—all are made with the help of chemical reactions. These new substances are better than their ingredients and are used for many purposes.

The most common irreversible chemical change that happens in our surroundings is rusting. Rusting happens when iron is exposed to oxygen for a long time. Iron oxide (FeO) is formed by a chemical reaction which is reddish-brown in colour.

Do It Yourself

Take a piece of iron that has rust on it. Rub it with a sand paper. You will notice that the rust is coming off, but iron is not restored to its original form. Once iron rusts, it becomes weak and loses its properties.

Rusted Iron Rods

Reversible Chemical Change

A reversible chemical change is turning water back into hydrogen and oxygen. This is done through the process of **electrolysis**. Water molecules are formed by bonding of two hydrogen and one oxygen atom. These atoms can be separated by the process of electrolysis.

In this process, electricity is used to break apart water at the molecular level. Electricity is passed through some water between two electrodes placed in the water. This process separates the hydrogen and oxygen and you can get the ingredients of water separately.

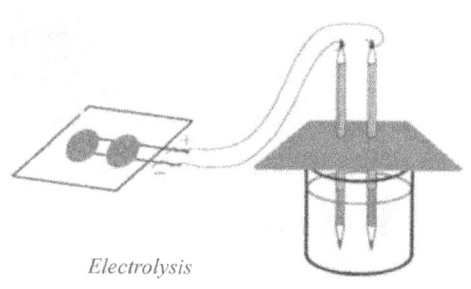

Electrolysis

The process of electrolysis is used to separate hydrogen and it is used as a **fuel**. This process was first formulated by **Michael Faraday** in **1820**.

Quick Facts

- Many elements and some compounds change from solids to liquids and from liquids to gases when heated and the reverse when cooled. Some substances, such as iodine and carbon dioxide go directly from solid to gas in a process called sublimation.

- Ferro magnetic materials can become magnetic. The process is reversible and does not affect the chemical composition.

- Crystals in metals have a major effect of the physical properties of the metal including strength and ductility. Crystal type, shape and size can be altered by physical hammering, rolling and by heat.

- Most solutions of salts and some compounds, such as sugars can be separated by evaporation. Others, such as mixtures or volatile liquids, such as low molecular weight alcohols, can be separated by fractional distillation.

Chapter - 12

ACIDS AND BASES

Every liquid that we see has either acidic or basic traits. One exception is distilled water. Water is neither acidic nor basic. The positive and negative ions in water are equal and cancel each other out. The ions in a solution make it *acidic or basic*.

A **pH scale** is used to measure how acidic or basic a solution is. The pH scale focuses on how many hydrogen ions and hydroxide ions are there in the solution. This scale goes from 0-14 with distilled water right in the middle, having its pH as 7.

Litmus Paper Test for Acids

Bases have a pH from 7-14 and acids have a pH from 0-7. Most liquids we see generally have a pH near 7. But in laboratories, you can find acids and bases that have high and low pH levels.

Acid

A solution that has an excess of H+ ions is an acid. An acid can be strong having a pH of 0-4 or weak having a pH of 3-6.

Properties of Acids

1. Acids taste sour. The word, acid comes from the Latin word, acere, which means sour.
2. Acids create hydrogen gas when they react with certain metal.
3. Acids react with bases to form salt and water.
4. Acids in an aqueous solution conduct electricity.
5. Acids change litmus from blue to red.

Examples of common acids are *citric acids* found in some *fruits* and *vegetables, vinegar, carbonic acid* and *lactic acid*.

Base

A solution that has an excess of OH+ ions is a base. A strong base has a very high pH from 10-14 and a weak base has a low pH from 8-10.

Litmus Paper Test in a Basic Solution

Properties of Bases

1. Bases taste bitter.
2. Bases feel slippery or soapy to touch.
3. Bases react with acids to form salts and water.
4. Bases in an aqueous solution conduct an electric current.
5. Bases don't change the colour of litmus. They can however change the acidic litmus, red, back to blue.

Some common bases are *detergents, soaps, household ammonia*, etc.

Detergent Powder Soap

pH Levels

The pH is the measure of the concentration of hydrogen ions in a solution. There are certain substances that change colour when they come in contact with an acid or a base. These substances are called *pH indicators*. Generally to determine the pH, paper soaked in certain pH indicators is used.

Litmus Paper

Litmus is a substance obtained from lichens, a fungus. It has a property of changing its colour to blue when it comes in contact with a base and red when it comes in contact with an acid. There is a scale on the packet of the litmus paper that indicates the colour assumed by the paper as a function of the pH.

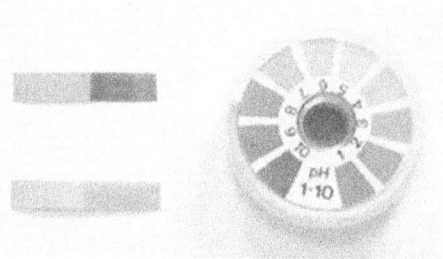
Litmus Papers and the Scales in them

To use a litmus paper, you have to dip one end of it into a solution and remove it immediately. The pH of the solution is determined by comparing its colour to the scale given on the packet.

pH Meter

A pH meter is an electronic instrument. It has a bulb which is sensitive to the presence of hydrogen ions in a solution. It has an analog meter to determine the pH of a solution. These instruments are more precise and convenient to use.

A pH Meter in Solution

Aqueous and Neutral Solutions

An aqueous solution is mainly water. A neutral solution is one that has a pH of 7. *It is neither acidic nor basic.*

Do it Yourself

Check the pH of different solutions found in your home. Take different bowls and put lemon juice, water, vinegar, soft drink and detergent mixed with water in them. Use a litmus paper to determine whether these solutions are acidic, basic or neutral.

Lemons

Detergent Powder

Vinegar

Soft Drink

Quick Facts

- Citric acid is present in many fruits, such as lemon, orange, pineapple, etc. These fruits are also called citrus fruits.
- An Acid Rain is the combination of sulphur dioxide and nitrogen dioxide from polluting clouds, from nuclear reactor and other fossil fuels. This then combines with oxygen and water and forms the rain clouds which consists of nitric acid and sulphuric acid.

Chapter - 13

SOLIDS

Solids are mostly hard because their molecules are tightly packed together. The tighter the molecules, the harder will be the substance. Solids can hold their shape until an external energy is applied to it.

The atoms in a solid cannot move around. In liquids and gases, the atoms and molecules can move around, but in solids, they remain stuck. This is a physical characteristic of a solid.

Solids can be made up of many things. They can contain one pure element or can be made up of various compounds. When there are a number of compounds that make up a solid, then it is called a **mixture**. Most **rocks** found on the earth are a **mixture of compounds**.

Mixture of Rocks, Sand and Water

Concrete is a very useful man-made solid mixture that is used on a very large scale in the construction of buildings. Although when made, **concrete** is a liquid but when it is allowed to settle down, it becomes one of the hardest man-made solids.

Types of Solids

Crystalline Solids

Solids in which the atoms, ions and molecules are arranged in a definite pattern and in a three-dimensional order are called **crystals**. When a solid is made up of a pure element and forms slowly, it can become a crystal. Not all pure substances can form crystals because it is a very delicate process. A crystal is simply an organised group of atoms and molecules. Each crystal has different properties and shapes.

Carbon is an element which can exist in more than one crystalline form. *Graphite* is an example of a crystal of carbon. Graphite is soft and is used as a conductor of electricity, in pencils and in strengthening of steel. *Diamond*, another crystal of carbon is one of the hardest known substance. It is used as an industrial cutting tool and in jewellery.

Common Uses of Crystals

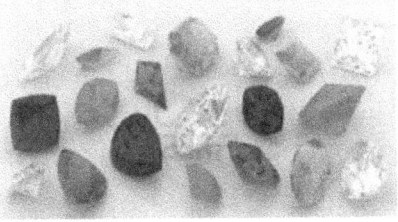

Precious Stones

Diamonds, rubies, sapphires and emeralds are all crystals that are used in jewellery as they are precious stones. They are highly valued and exist in a very limited quantity on the earth. In recent years, chemists have been able to make some of these crystals in laboratories with successful results.

Amorphous Solids

A Glass Window

In amorphous solids, particles are not arranged in any particular arrangement. Also, shapeless solids are called amorphous solids. Most solids are found in the amorphous form. plastic materials and gels are amorphous solids.

Properties and Uses of Solids

1. Physical Properties of Solids

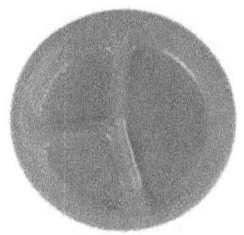
A Plastic Plate

Solids retain their shapes until or unless an external force is applied on them. They are hard to touch and cannot be compressed. Therefore, solids are used in places where there is a need to support something.

Solids are everywhere around us. The chair we sit on, cars and bikes in which we travel, mobile phone, computers all are solids. They are used for a variety of purposes.

Chair   *Mobile*   *Computer*

2. Mechanical Properties of Solids

Mechanical properties include elasticity, ductility, compressive strength, etc. Rubber is an elastic. Its shape can be changed when it is heated. Rubber is used in tyres, shoes and erasers, etc.

A Spacecraft

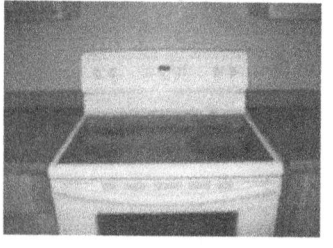
A Glass-top Stove

Glass-ceramics are used in counter-top cooking as they exhibit excellent mechanical properties. Polymers, ceramics and metal composite materials are used in aircraft and spacecraft exteriors.

3. Electrical Properties of Solids

Electrical properties of solids include how well a substance conducts or resists electricity. **Semiconductors** act somewhere in between. Copper is a good **conductor** of electricity and is used to make electrical wires. Wood is a poor conductor of electricity or an **insulator** and therefore, it is recommended to use a wooden stool when working with electrical wires.

Copper Electrical Wire

4. Thermal Properties of Solids

Utensils

Thermal properties of solids include how well a substance conducts heat. Some solids are good conductors of electricity and some are not. Iron, steel, aluminium, etc are good conductors and are therefore used in cooking utensils. Plastic and rubber are bad conductors of heat and are therefore used in making gloves to handle hot materials.

5. Magnetic Properties of Solids

As an electron is a charged particle, the circular motion of the electric charge causes the electron to act as a tiny electromagnet. *Iron, nickel and cobalt are magnetic solids. Iron is used to make magnets which are then used for various purposes.*

A Magnet

Quick Facts

- In solids, the atoms are fixed in location, but they constantly vibrate and vibrate faster with more heat. Thus, solids have a fixed shape.

- In liquids, the atoms are moving, bumping into each other but sticking to each other only momentarily. Thus, liquids take on the shape of their containers.

- In gases, the atoms are moving with high speed and frequently bump into each other without sticking. Therefore, gases also take the shape of their containers.

- Solids are of various types. Metals, their alloys, some non-metals, and ionic chemical compounds are crystalline in form. Some solids, e.g., chalk and clay, have no regular structure and are called amorphous. Substances, such as pitch and resin are called semisolids; these are actually very viscid liquids, but their flow or change of shape is so slow at ordinary temperatures as to be scarcely discernible by the human eye. Properties in which solids differ from one another include density, hardness, malleability, ductility, elasticity, brittleness, and tensile strength.

Chapter - 14

LIQUIDS

Liquid molecules are a little loosely packed. They can move around, and therefore liquids flow. Liquids have a fixed density but no fixed shape. A liquid can either be made up of a single substance or of two or more compounds. Liquids when made up of two or more compounds are called **solutions**.

A liquid generally takes the shape of its container. When you fill a glass with water, the water will first fill up the bottom and then rise up. It fills in the bottom first because of gravity.

Liquids are hard to compress. When we compress a substance, we take a certain amount of it and force it into a smaller space. To be able to get compressed, the atoms should have enough space between each other. Gases are very easily compressed as their atoms are far apart, while solids are the most difficult because their atoms are tightly packed. In liquids too, the atoms are tightly packed but not like solids.

Liquid particles are bound firmly but not rigidly. When heat is applied the molecules start moving faster and faster and when it reaches its boiling point, the liquids will change into a gas. In the opposite way, if the temperature is decreased, the molecules of a liquid will come closer together and become slow, this will change the liquid into a solid.

Uses of Liquids

Liquids have a lot of uses in our daily lives. Their uses depend upon their significant characteristics. Liquids are largely used as *lubricants, solvents,* and *coolants.*

Lubricant

Grease

A substance that is used to reduce friction when applied to a surface as a coating, particularly in moving parts of vehicles and machines is called a lubricant. *Oil* and *grease* are used in many machines as lubricants.

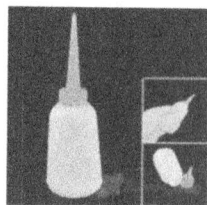
Machine Oil

Solvent

Adhesive

A solvent is a substance in which another substance is dissolved. Liquids are used as solvents to dissolve other liquids or solids in them. After dissolving another substance in a liquid, it becomes a solution. Solutions have a variety of uses. Some of the common solutions are adhesives, paints and sealants. Body fluids are also solutions that have *water* as their base.

Paint

Coolant

A coolant is an agent that produces cooling, generally a fluid that draws off heat. Liquids have a good thermal conductivity. Therefore *liquids* are more favourable to be used as coolants in machinery. In this process, either the liquid is made to travel through the heated part or the heated part is dipped into the liquid.

Radiator of a Car

Surface Tension

Have you ever tried to dive into a swimming pool and then fallen flat on the water instead? If yes, then you know about surface tension. It is because of surface tension that you get hurt and it feels as if the water has hit you back.

Drops of Water on a Leaf

Surface tension is the ability of a liquid to resist an external force. This happens because in a liquid, each molecule is pulling towards other molecules in all directions. But the molecules right at the surface are pulling in directions other than the upward direction. This creates a tension at the surface.

Viscosity

Some liquids flow freely, while some others don't. This depends on the viscosity of the liquid. In simple terms, viscosity is the thickness or the internal friction of a liquid. *Honey has a high viscosity* and therefore, it is thick, while *water has a low viscosity* and therefore, flows more freely.

A Drop of Honey Falls Slowly than Water

Quick Facts

- Liquids can flow and their atoms are loosely packed. This does not mean that they are not strong. Water flowing in rivers can carve out rocks. In many places on the earth, rivers have carved out great valleys and canyons. The Grand Canyon is one such natural structure which has been carved out by the Colorado River.

- Water settling on a leaf in the form of a drop is an example of surface tension. Water sticks weakly to the leaf and strongly to its own molecules and therefore, it forms a spherical shape or a drop.
- Roughly 70 percent of an adult's body is made up of water.
- At birth, water accounts for approximately 80 percent of an infant's body weight.
- A healthy person can drink about three gallons (48 cups) of water per day. However, drinking too much water too quickly can lead to water intoxication. Water intoxication occurs when water dilutes the sodium level in the bloodstream and causes an imbalance of water in the brain.
- While the daily recommended amount of water is eight cups per day, not all of this water must be consumed in the liquid form because nearly every food or drink item provides some water to the body.

Chapter - 15

GASES

Gases are all around us. *All the air around us is gas.* The atoms in a gas are very far apart and are full of energy. They keep bouncing around. *Gases neither have a definite shape nor a definite volume.*

Gases can fill a container of any size or shape. When you fill a balloon with a gas, it spreads to the whole of the balloon. If we fill a balloon with a liquid then the liquids always settles at the bottom first.

Vapour and gas is the same thing. Although the term vapour is generally used for gases that are usually found as liquids. Gases like carbon dioxide and nitrogen are found in the gaseous state at room temperature therefore they will not be called vapours. Whereas when water turns into a gas it is called water vapour.

A Balloon Filled with Air

The atoms and molecules in gases are spread out as much as they can be. Gases have a lot of energy in them. They can float about and get into a tiny amount of space.

Gases can be compressed with little pressure. Compressed air is in a spray bottle and gets

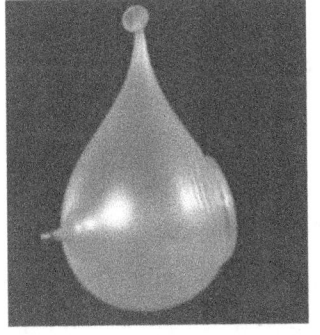

A Balloon Half Filled with Air

released when we press the bottle. When we open soft drink cans we can hear the gas escaping from it, this is also gas compressed in the can.

A pure gas can made up of individual atoms or molecules made up of one type of atoms like neon or compound molecules made from a variety of atoms like car dioxide. A gas mixture can contain a variety of different gas atoms like air.

Deodorant Bottle

A Soft Drink Can

The air we breathe contains 78% nitrogen, 21% oxygen, 1% argon, .03% carbon dioxide and small measures of other gases.

Gases are generally invisible to the eye. You can feel the presence of a gas sometimes by its smell, or the sound or if it has a particular colour.

Physical Characteristics of Gases

Density and Viscosity

Compared to liquids and solids, gases have a very low density and viscosity. They flow easily and take up space inside the container they are. The atoms spread out and cover the whole container.

Pressure

The term, pressure in gases is referred to the amount of force the gas exerts on the surface area of a container. Gas pressure is measured in **Pascal**.

Temperature

The temperature of a gas can be determined by us by simply feeling if one gas is hotter than the other. In a hot gas, the molecules move faster than the molecules in a cold gas. The temperature is more because the molecules in a hotter gas move faster.

Atmospheric Pressure

The atmosphere of the earth is made up of many gases. All these gases exert a pressure on everything on the earth's surface. This pressure is called the atmospheric pressure. In the early 17th century, **Evangelista Torricelli** invented a **barometer** to measure the pressure that our atmosphere exerts on us. Torricelli's invention contradicted the belief of people that air is weightless.

A Barometer

Evangelista Torricelli

Quick Facts

- The ozone layer in the earth's atmosphere protects the earth from the sun's harmful Ultraviolet rays. Ozone has three oxygen atoms bound together. The Ozone layer is a part of the Stratosphere and it is not very thick. The Ozone layer is thicker near the equator and thinner near the poles.

- It has been observed that the ozone layer is depleting. Since it protects the earth from harmful UV rays that can cause skin cancer, the ozone layer depletion is a cause for concern. The depletion has been greatest at high altitudes and mostly notable in Antarctica during winter.

- The air we breathe on earth is made up of different gases. It contains around 78% nitrogen, 21% oxygen, 1% argon and a small amount of other gases.
- Natural gas contains mostly methane. It is used as a fuel to generate electricity and is common in homes, where it can be used for heating, cooking and other purposes.
- The gas pressure is measured in pascals.
- The helium balloons you get at parties and carnivals float because helium is lighter than the air surrounding it.
- Noble gases are a group of chemical elements that are very stable under normal conditions. Naturally occurring noble gases include helium, neon, argon, krypton, xenon and radon.

Exercises

I. Answer the following questions.

1. What is matter and what are the four main types of matter that exist on the earth? Describe briefly.

2. What are the many different properties based on which materials can be classified? Explain them briefly.

3. Explain the following terms briefly with one example each. Melting, Freezing, Evaporation and Condensation.

4. What is an atom and what is it made of? Explain with the help of a diagram.

5. What is Chemical Bonding and what are the two different types of chemical bonds?

6. Define Mass, Volume and Density. How are they measured? Explain their relationship with the help of a formula.

7. What is a molecule? Explain the structure of a water molecule and the bond formed between the atoms of a water molecule.

8. What are elements and how are they arranged in a periodic table?

9. What are metals and non-metals? Explain with two of their properties and examples.

10. What do you understand by the physical and chemical properties of elements? Explain with the help of an example.

II. Fill in the blanks with suitable words.

1. When different elements bond together through a chemical reaction, they form _____.
2. _____ are formed when elements are mixed together and no bonding takes place.
3. Examples of compounds are _____ and _____.
4. To get pure iron, elements, such as iron and oxygen have to be separated and this is done in a _____.
5. The two different types of compounds are: _____ and _____.
6. When a mixture is formed, no energy is either _____ or _____.
7. In a sugar-water solution, sugar is called the _____ and water is called the _____.
8. A _____ is a mixture of two substances which do not dissolve completely.
9. _____ of iron takes a long time, while cooking creates chemical reactions in minutes.
10. A _____ change may change the size, shape or colour of a substance, but does not change its composition.

III. Match the two columns correctly.

A	B
1. A reversible chemical change is	with bases to form salt and water.
2. A pH scale is used to measure	sulphur dioxide and nitrogen dioxide from polluting clouds.

3. Acids taste sour and they react
4. An Acid Rain is the combination of
5. Solids are mostly hard

how acidic or basic a solution is.
because their molecules are tightly packed together.
turning water into hydrogen and oxygen.

IV. Multiple Choice Questions (MCQs)

1. A solid in which the atoms, ions and molecules are arranged in a definite pattern and in a three-dimensional order are called
   a. Crystals
   b. Stones
   c. Semi-solids
   d. Metals

2. A liquid generally takes the shape of its
   a. Molecules
   b. Container
   c. Atoms
   d. Volume

3. Thermal properties of solids include how well a substance
   a. Conducts Electricity
   b. Conducts Force
   c. Conducts Heat

4. Window glass, plastic materials and gels are examples of
   a. Amorphous liquids
   b. Transparent solids
   c. Amorphous solids

5. Litmus is a substance obtained from lichens, which is a/an
   a. Algae
   b. Fungi
   c. Bacteria
   d. Virus

6. Surface tension is the ability of a liquid to resist an
    a. External force   b. Internal force
    c. Both Internal & External force
7. The ozone layer in the earth's atmosphere protects the earth from the sun's harmful
    a. Ultraviolet rays b. Infrared rays
    c. Ultrasonic rays   d. Cosmic rays
8. Acids change litmus paper from blue to
    a. Orange   b. Green
    c. Red   e. Yellow

Glossary

Electromagnetic Radiation: Radiation originating from visible light, radio waves, x-rays, etc.

Compressible: To press together, or to cause to become a solid mass

Combine: Join together

Definite: Particular shape, volume, etc.

Rigid: Inflexible, Firm, Fixed

Container: Vessel

Atmosphere: Environment

Ionizing: To separate or change into ions

Conductive: Denoting or having the property of conduction

Properties: Features

Fluorescent: Strikingly bright

Lightning: A brilliant shark or discharge of light during thunderstorm

Condensate: A substance formed by condensation

Super-unexcited: Super-inactive

Blob: A globule of liquid, bubble

Element: Substance, component

Vacuum: A space entirely devoid of matter

Plasma: A highly ionized gas containing an equal number of positive ions and electrons

Pressure: The exertion of force upon a surface by an object, fluid, etc.

Temperature: A measure of warmth or coldness of an object of a living body

Density: The state or quality of being dense, or mass per unit volume

Vapour: Particles of moisture or other substances suspended in air, substance in a gaseous state

Brittle: Hard, rough, rigid

Transparent: Admitting the passage light

Freezing: Chilled, to become hardened into a solid

Boiling: Steaming or reaching the boiling point

Melting: To become a liquid

Flexibility: Capable of being bent, can easily undergo change

Rigidity: Stiff or inflexible

Evaproation: The process of changing a liquid to gas or vapour

Galaxy: A large system of stars held together by mutual gravitation

Microscope: An optical instrument having a magnifying lens

Periodic Table: A table of elements containing metals and non-metals

Atom Bomb: A type of bomb in which energy is provided by nuclear fission

CAREER & BUSINESS MANAGEMENT
(कॅरियर एण्ड बिजनेस मैनेजमेंट)

JOB RELATED
(नौकरी सम्बन्धी)

Contact us at sales@vspublishers.com

Quiz Books (प्रश्नोत्तरी की पुस्तकें) | MYSTERIES (रहस्य)

DRAWING BOOKS (ड्राइंग बुक्स) | BIOGRAPHIES (आत्म कथा)

 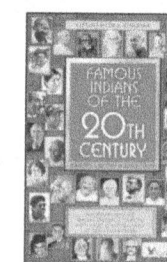

QUOTES/SAYINGS (उद्धरण/सूक्तियाँ)

PUZZLES (पहेलियाँ) | ACTIVITIES BOOK (एक्टिविटीज बुक)

Contact us at sales@vspublishers.com

www.ingramcontent.com/pod-product-compliance
Lightning Source LLC
Chambersburg PA
CBHW080448110426
42743CB00016B/3323